Food

PASTA

Louise Spilsbury

www.heinemann.co.uk/library
Visit our website to find out more information about Heinemann Library books.

To order:
 Phone 44 (0) 1865 888066
 Send a fax to 44 (0) 1865 314091
 Visit the Heinemann Bookshop at www.heinemann.co.uk/library to browse our catalogue and order online.

First published in Great Britain by Heinemann Library,
Halley Court, Jordan Hill, Oxford OX2 8EJ
a division of Reed Educational and Professional Publishing Ltd.
Heinemann is a registered trademark of Reed Educational & Professional Publishing Ltd.

OXFORD MELBOURNE AUCKLAND
JOHANNESBURG BLANTYRE GABORONE
IBADAN PORTSMOUTH (NH) USA CHICAGO

Designed by Celia Floyd
Illustrated by Barry Atkinson
Originated by Ambassador Litho Ltd
Printed by South China Printing Co in Hong Kong.

ISBN 0 431 12703 4 (hardback)
05 04 03 02
10 9 8 7 6 5 4 3 2

ISBN 0 431 12713 1 (paperback)
06 05 04 03 02
10 9 8 7 6 5 4 3 2 1

British Library Cataloguing in Publication Data
Spilsbury, Louise
    Pasta. – (Food)
    1. Pasta products 2. Cookery (Pasta)
    I. Title
    641.3'8

Acknowledgements
The Publishers would like to thank the following for permission to reproduce photographs:
AKG p.8; Anthony Blake Photo Library p.10, 16; Gareth Boden pp.5, 6, 7, 22, 23, 28; Bruce Coleman Collection/Dr Eckart Pott p.12; Corbis pp.17, 20, /Philip de Bay p.9, /Owen Franken p.18, John Heseltine p.14, /Vittoriano Rastelli pp. 15, 19, 21; Robert Harding p.4; Tony Stone Images pp.11, 24, 25.

Cover photograph reproduced with permission of Gareth Boden.

Every effort has been made to contact copyright holders of any material reproduced in this book. Any omissions will be rectified in subsequent printings if notice is given to the Publisher.

CONTENTS

What is pasta? 4

Kinds of pasta 6

In the past 8

Around the world 10

Looking at wheat 12

Fresh and dried 14

Making pasta 16

Cutting and shaping 18

Drying and packing 20

Eating pasta 22

Good for you 24

Healthy eating 26

Pasta salad recipe 28

Glossary 30

More books to read 32

Index 32

Words written in bold, **like this**, are explained in the Glossary.

WHAT IS PASTA?

Pasta is an important food for many people across the world. In Italy most people eat pasta every day.

Pasta is made from **flour** and water. These are its main **ingredients**. They are mixed to a paste, sometimes with egg or oil. The word pasta means paste in Italian.

KINDS OF PASTA

Pasta can be made with **wholemeal** or white **flour**. Other foods, like tomato or spinach, may be added to give a different colour and flavour.

white   wholemeal

tomato

spinach

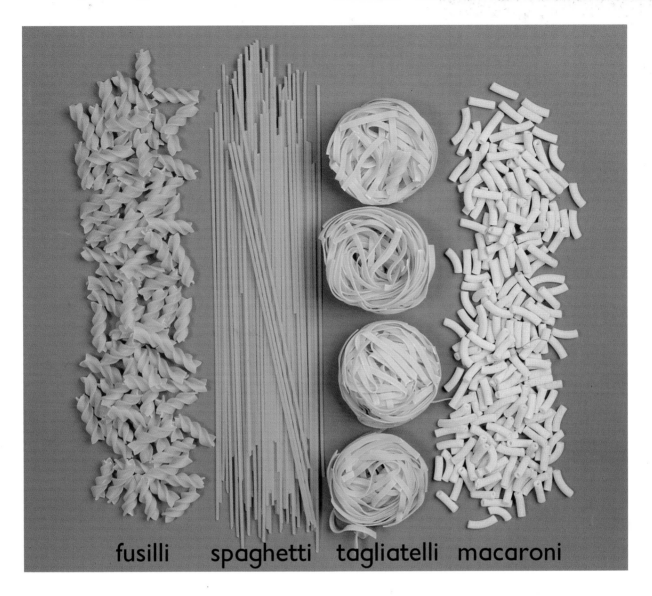

fusilli   spaghetti   tagliatelli   macaroni

You can buy pasta in hundreds of
shapes and sizes. The different kinds
of pasta all have their own names.
These names are usually Italian.

IN THE PAST

Pasta comes from Italy. Some people believe that the famous Italian traveller Marco Polo brought the recipe for pasta back from China about 700 years ago. He travelled back in a ship like one of these.

Many Italians say that pasta was eaten in Italy before this time. Poor people, like those in this painting, ate a lot of pasta because it was cheap.

AROUND THE WORLD

Today pasta is eaten all over the world. In many countries spaghetti is one of the most popular kinds of pasta.

In China, Japan and Korea many people eat noodles. Noodles are made from **wheat** or other kinds of **flour**, and are similar to spaghetti.

LOOKING AT WHEAT

Pasta **flour** is made from **grains** of **wheat**. A machine crushes the grains into a powder. The grains grow at the top of the **stalk** on a wheat plant.

grains

stalk

leaf

White flour is made from the **endosperm** (inside) of the wheat grain. **Wholemeal** flour is brown. It is made using the layer of **bran** as well. This is a grain of wheat.

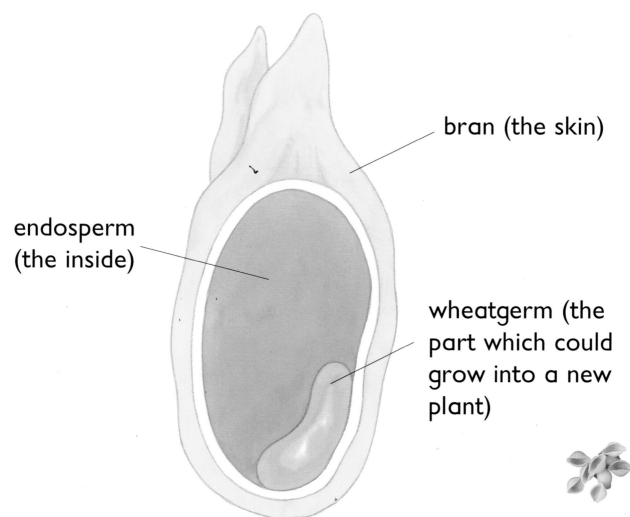

bran (the skin)

endosperm (the inside)

wheatgerm (the part which could grow into a new plant)

FRESH AND DRIED

Some people make fresh pasta at home. They mix **flour**, water and egg into a thick **dough**. They push it through a machine to make pasta shapes. You can also buy fresh pasta in shops.

Most people use **dried** pasta, which is made in **factories**. You can keep it for a long time before you cook it. Freshly made pasta does not keep for long.

MAKING PASTA

Dried pasta is made by machines. Computers tell them what to do. First the machines measure out the correct amounts of **flour** and water.

The flour and water are put into large tubs. Machines mix and **knead** the flour and water together to make a thick **dough**.

CUTTING AND SHAPING

When the **dough** is ready, it goes into a pressing machine. This machine presses the dough through metal plates with holes in them.

To make spaghetti, the holes are round and very small. The shape and size of the holes are what makes the different kinds of pasta.

DRYING AND PACKING

The pasta is **dried** using blasts of hot air. Then it is checked and measured so it is ready to be packed.

Finally, a machine weighs the dried pasta and drops it into packets. The labels on the packets tell **consumers** all about the pasta inside.

EATING PASTA

People don't usually eat pasta by itself. It is cooked for 5 to 12 minutes in boiling water. Then a vegetable, cheese or meat sauce is poured over the top.

Some pasta is shaped to hold fillings inside. Ravioli are little pasta parcels stuffed with meat or cheese. Cannelloni are pasta tubes baked with fillings inside.

ravioli   cannelloni

GOOD FOR YOU

Pasta is a **carbohydrate**. This means it is a kind of food that gives us **energy**. We use up energy in everything we do.

People who do a lot of sport often eat pasta. The energy pasta gives them lasts a long time. Pasta gives runners **stamina**.

HEALTHY EATING

You need to eat different kinds of food to keep well. This food pyramid shows how much of each different food you need.

Pasta is in the group at the bottom of the pyramid. You need to eat some of the things in this group every day.

You should eat some of the foods shown in the middle every day, too. You need only very small amounts of the foods at the top.

The food in each part of the pyramid helps your body in different ways.

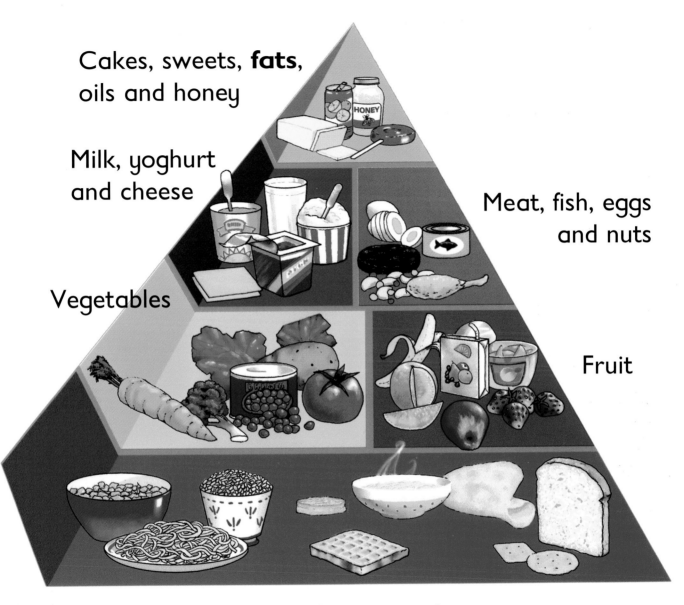

Cakes, sweets, **fats**, oils and honey

Milk, yoghurt and cheese

Meat, fish, eggs and nuts

Vegetables

Fruit

Bread, **cereals**, rice and pasta

PASTA SALAD RECIPE

1 To cook the pasta, put it into a pan of boiling water. Boil it for about 12 minutes (check time needed on the packet).

2 Drain the pasta through a **colander** and leave it in a bowl until it is cold.

You will need:
- 225g pasta
- water
- 175g cheese
- 1 red pepper
- half a cucumber
- salad dressing

colander

Ask an adult to help you!

3 Cut the cheese, red pepper and cucumber into small pieces. Add these to the pasta.

4 Stir in a large spoonful of salad dressing to taste, and serve.

GLOSSARY

bran brown skin that covers a wheat grain

carbohydrate kind of food that gives us energy

cereal grains like wheat, rye, corn and rice that are used for foods like flour, bread and breakfast cereals

colander metal or plastic bowl with holes in it. It can be used to separate pasta from the water it was cooked in.

consumers people who buy things that they need or want, like food

dough soft, thick mixture made with flour and water

dried some kinds of food are dried out before being packed and sold. This means they can be kept for a long time before they are used.

endosperm the inside of a grain of wheat

energy all living things need energy to live, move and grow. Our energy comes from the food we eat.

factories very large buildings where people and machines make things, such as toys or shoes, or food such as pasta

fat type of food. It is not healthy to eat or drink too many fatty foods.

flour food made by grinding the grains of some plants like wheat into a powder

grain seed of a cereal plant

ingredients foods such as flour and oil, mixed or cooked together to make another food, like pasta

knead pulling and squeezing dough

stalk part of a plant that holds the leaves and flowers up above the ground

stamina the energy to keep going for a long time, such as in a race or long swim

steam when water is heated (such as when it is boiled in a pan), some of it turns into steam that you can see in the air. Steam is very hot and damp.

wheat kind of plant. The grain (seed) of the wheat plant is crushed to make flour for bread or pasta making.

wholemeal wholemeal flour is made by crushing the whole of the wheat grain, including the bran

MORE BOOKS TO READ

Senses: Tasting, K. Hartley, C. Macro, P. Taylor, Heinemann Library, 2000

Plants: Plants and Us, Angela Royston, Heinemann Library, 2000

Body Wise – Why Do I Feel Hungry? Sharon Cromwell, Heinemann Library, 1998

Step into Italy, Fred Martin, Heinemann Library, 1998

Let's Explore Keeping Healthy, Franklin Watts

INDEX

carbohydrates   24, 30

consumers   21, 30

dough   14, 17, 18, 30

dried pasta   15, 16, 17, 18, 19, 20, 21, 30

energy   24, 25

flavours   6

flour   5, 6, 11, 12, 14, 16, 17, 31

fresh pasta   14, 15

ingredients   5, 31

names   7

noodles   11

shapes   18, 19

stamina   25, 31

wheat plants   12, 13, 31